WILD WICKED WONDERFUL

TOP 10: EATERS

By Virginia Loh-Hagan

45th Parallel Press

Published in the United States of America by Cherry Lake Publishing
Ann Arbor, Michigan
www.cherrylakepublishing.com

Content Adviser: Stephen Ditchkoff, Professor of Wildlife Ecology and Management, Auburn University, Alabama
Reading Adviser: Marla Conn, ReadAbility, Inc.
Book Designer: Melinda Millward

Photo Credits: Photo Credits:
© Schnappschusshelge/Dreamstime.com, cover, 1, 26; ©Naraka/Shutterstock Images, 5; ©ivkuzmin / iStockphoto, 6; ©Janossy Gergely/Shutterstock Images, 6; © Vilainecrevette/Dreamstime.com, 6; ©Cuson/Shutterstock Images, 7; ©nattanan726/ Shutterstock Images, 8; ©chakkrachai nicharat/Shutterstock Images, 10; ©Dr. Morley Read/Shutterstock Images, 11; ©khazari/ Shutterstock Images, 12; ©kungverylucky/Shutterstock Images, 14; ©duangnapa_b/Shutterstock Images, 14; ©tatianaput/ Shutterstock Images, 14; ©ostill/Shutterstock Images, 15; © Maieru Alina/Dreamstime.com, 16; ©Dennis Burns/ iStockphoto, 16; ©Richard Whitcombe/Shutterstock Images, 16; ©RHIMAGE/Shutterstock Images, 17; ©Juan Gaertner/Shutterstock Images, 18, 19; © Iliuta Goean/Dreamstime.com, 20; © Maya Paulin/Dreamstime.com, 20; ©James A Dawson/Shutterstock Images, 21; ©Aigars Reinholds/Shutterstock Images, 22; © Altaoosthuizen/Dreamstime.com, 23; ©Anneka/Shutterstock Images, 24; ©Dirk Ercken/Shutterstock Images, 24, 25; ©Doug Schnurr/Shutterstock Images, 24; ©toos/ iStockphoto, 26; ©DragoNika/ Shutterstock Images, 26; © L Kennedy / Alamy Stock Photo, 27; ©Jan-Nor Photography/Shutterstock Images, 28; ©ajman/ Shutterstock Images, 29; © Luis Tejo/Dreamstime.com, 30; ©Stanislav Duben/Shutterstock Images, 31

Graphic Element Credits: © tukkki/Shutterstock Images, back cover, front cover, multiple interior pages; © paprika/Shutterstock Images, back cover, front cover, multiple interior pages; © Silhouette Lover/Shutterstock Images, multiple interior pages

45th Parallel Press is an imprint of Cherry Lake Publishing.

Library of Congress Cataloging-in-Publication Data

Names: Loh-Hagan, Virginia, author.
   Title: Top 10 : eaters / by Virginia Loh-Hagan.
Other titles: Top ten : eaters | Eaters
Description: Ann Arbor, Michigan : Cherry Lake Publishing, [2016] | Series: Wild wicked wonderful
Identifiers: LCCN 2015026851| ISBN 9781634705035 (hardcover) | ISBN
9781634706230 (pbk.) | ISBN 9781634705639 (pdf) | ISBN 9781634706834 (ebook)
Subjects: LCSH: Animals—Food—Juvenile literature. | Animals—Miscellanea—Juvenile literature.
Classification: LCC QL756.5 .L64 2016 | DDC 591.5—dc23
LC record available at http://lccn.loc.gov/2015026851

Printed in the United States of America
Corporate Graphics

About the Author

Dr. Virginia Loh-Hagan is an author, university professor, former classroom teacher, and curriculum designer. She loves to eat. She can eat twice her size in food. She lives in San Diego with her very tall husband and very naughty dogs. To learn more about her, visit www.virginialoh.com.

TABLE OF CONTENTS

INTRODUCTION

Animals need to eat. They hunt. They chew. They **digest**. Digest means to take in food. Bodies break down food. They take in the food bits. They get rid of bits they don't need.

Animals eat to **survive**. Survive means to stay alive. They need food. Food gives them energy. Food builds muscles. Food keeps their organs working. Food keeps them healthy.

Some animals are **prey**. Prey are animals hunted for food. Some animals are **predators**. Predators are hunters. They eat prey.

Some animals are extreme eaters. They have strange eating habits. They have strange eating styles. They're the most exciting eaters in the animal world!

Animals can be both prey and predators.

Chapter one

SLOTHS

Sloths live in jungles. They live in Central and South America. They eat a **diet** of leaves. A diet is what animals eat. Sloths don't need a lot of energy. They have half as many muscles as other animals their size. They don't need a lot of muscles.

They spend their lives upside down. They hang by their claws. Their claws are long and curved. They have strong grips. They don't fall down.

Their bodies are made for hanging. Their organs are upside down. They can't walk upright on the ground.

Sloths hang almost all the time. Even after death.

Some sloths are picky eaters. They only eat leaves from a few trees.

Sloths have long tongues. Their tongues stick out 12 inches (30.5 centimeters). They use their tongues. They use them to grab things. They can turn their heads. They turn their heads almost all the way around. They eat without moving much.

They're slow. They don't move much. So they don't need much food. They can live on a small amount.

They're too slow to hunt. They don't look for food. They save energy. They eat leaves close to them. They also eat bugs and eggs.

Sloths have slow digestion systems. They only need to use the bathroom once a week. They do this on the ground.

HUMANS DO WHAT?!?

Humans do weird things. Some participate in dung-spitting contests. Dung is animal poop. This is a sport. The sport began in 1994. But it started with tribal hunters. The hunters couldn't catch fast antelope. They saw their dung. They were bored. They spit dung to pass the time. Now, dung-spitting is popular. It's practiced in South Africa. There's a yearly world championship. People use antelope dung. They use small, hard pieces of dung. They dip it in alcohol. This helps clean the dung. They put it in their mouths. They spit. The winner is the person who spits the farthest. Judges measure where the dung lands. Shaun van Rensburg set a world record in 2006. He spit the farthest dung. He spit dung 51.05 feet (15.5 m).

Chapter two

TERMITES

Termites love eating wood. They look for dead trees. They look for rotting trees. They get rid of these trees. They eat them.

They may be tiny. But they can eat tall trees. They can eat big trees. They eat together. There are lots of termites. For every human, there's half a ton of termites. African termite queens produce 30,000 eggs every day!

Termites also eat dead wood from houses. They cause $1 billion worth of damage a year. One termite group can eat more than 150 feet (45.7 meters) of wood a year. Ten groups can eat a whole house in seven years.

In the wild, termites are nature's destruction crew.

Termites have special stomachs that digest wood.

Wood produces a lot of energy. But it's hard to eat. Wood has special fibers. Humans can't digest wood. But termites can.

Termites have special stomachs. Tiny things live in their stomachs. They help termites digest. These things can only be seen with a **microscope**. A microscope is a a tool with a lens. It makes small things big.

Termites have special mouthparts. Their mouthparts are strong. They chew up wood. They chew bit by bit.

Termites are smart. They survive by eating wood. Not many animals eat wood. Termites don't have much competition.

DID YOU KNOW...?

- Humans eat a pound of bugs in a lifetime! Bugs get trapped in processed foods.

- Sloth bears eat termites. They dig them out. They have dangerous claws. Their claws are like curved blades. Sloth bears are nasty when they fight. They rip faces off. They leave victims half-eaten.

- Parrot fish can change genders. They can be males. They can be females. They can also change their colors and patterns.

- In one year, humans shed 1.5 pounds (24 ounces) of skin. Eighty percent of floating dust is dead skin. Dust mites are happy eaters. Ten percent of pillows are dust mites and their droppings.

- Some spas use cleaner fish. The cleaner fish clean dry skin off feet. There are three types of cleaner fish. Strikers eat the skin. Suckers draw blood. Healers spit on the cuts.

- Native Colombians use poison dart frogs' poison. They tip their blowgun darts with the poison.

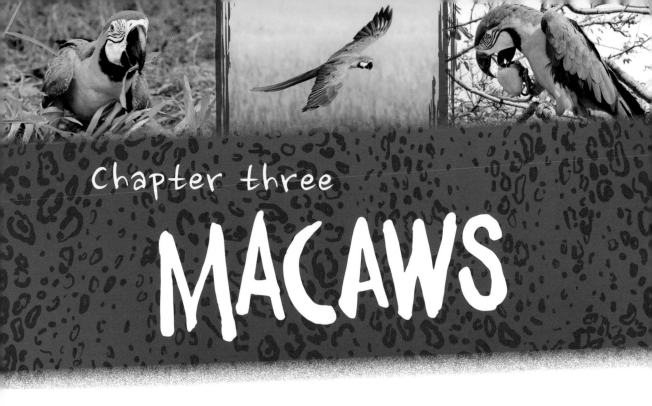

Chapter three

MACAWS

Macaws are special parrots. They live by riverbanks. They live in South America. They eat clay. They eat a tenth of their weight each day.

They like eating clay. But they also have to eat clay. Clay keeps them alive. They like to eat poisonous seeds. Many plants add poison to their seeds. These plants want to protect themselves.

Macaws found a way to eat poisonous seeds. Clay has **minerals**. Minerals are special crystals. The clay binds

Macaws visit riverbanks and cliffs made of clay.

with the poisons. The minerals cancel out the poisons. Eating clay allows macaws to digest poisonous seeds.

chapter four
PARROT FiSH

Parrot fish have large front teeth. The teeth are joined together. They look like a parrot's beak.

Parrot fish use their beaks. They break off tiny pieces of **coral**. Coral are sea animals. They stay in one place. They're hard as rock. They look like underwater cacti. Many animals live in coral.

Parrot fish eat 4,000 mouthfuls of coral every day. They grind it. They chew it. They have special teeth. These teeth are in the back of their throats. Parrot fish eat living things on the coral.

Every day, parrot fish chew 6 pounds (2.7 kilograms) of rock.

Rocks pass through their bodies. Parrot fish poop out sand. They make 200 pounds (90.7 kg) of fine white sand each year.

Chapter five

DUST MITES

Dust mites are really small. They can only be seen with a microscope. They have eight legs. They're **scavengers**. Scavengers feed on dead animals or plants. Dust mites eat dead skin. They poop out digested skin.

Humans make a lot of skin cells. Humans lose more than 4,000 skin cells every five seconds. Humans shed over a million skin cells every hour.

Dust mites can live anywhere. But they love humans' beds. A human sleeps with two million dust mites. Dust mites live in carpets. They live in furniture.

Dust mites eat more of us than any other creature on Earth.

Dust mites have simple guts. They don't have stomachs.
They have pouches. They have hollow organs.

Chapter six

CLEANER FISH

Cleaner fish are little fish. They eat anything in the water. They **groom** other fish. They clean other fish. They eat dead skin. They eat **parasites**. Parasites are tiny living things. They live on animals. They eat animals. They can cause sickness.

One cleaner fish can eat 1,200 parasites in a day. They can clean more than 2,500 fish. They help ocean animals.

Cleaner fish work in an area of the **reef**. A reef is a ridge of coral rocks. Ocean animals come into their area. They stay still. They spread their fins. Cleaner fish clean them. They even clean sharks. They clean the inside of sharks' mouths.

Cleaner fish operate an underwater car wash.

Chapter seven

DUNG BEETLES

Dung beetles eat **dung**. Dung is poop. A pile of fresh dung attracts more than 1,600 beetles. Dung beetles can eat it all. They do it in less than two hours.

Sometimes, they don't finish the dung. They roll it into a ball. They save it for later. They hide the ball underground. They protect it from other dung beetles. They also use the ball to hide their eggs. The dung ball is a safe place. Baby dung beetles grow up in this ball. They eat whenever they want.

Dung beetles are helpful. They clean up animal waste. Without them, there'd be a lot of poop.

Dung beetles are nature's walking waste disposal units.

Chapter eight
POiSON DART FROGS

Poison dart frogs live in jungles. They live in Central and South America. They're the world's most poisonous animals. They're 25 times more poisonous than cobras. Their skin is poisonous. Their poison can kill 10 humans.

They eat ants. They eat spiders. They eat bugs with poison. They use their prey's poison. They change it. They add it to the poison on their skin.

They have super eyesight. Their tongues are sticky and long. They dart their tongues out. They catch their prey.

Poison dart frogs are small. They're about 0.6 inches (1.5 cm).

Poison dart frogs are very colorful. This warns predators. Predators know not to touch these frogs.

Chapter nine

MEERKATS

Meerkats live in the Kalahari Desert in Africa. They love to eat scorpions. Scorpions are related to spiders. Scorpions have **pincers**, or claws. These are for grabbing and holding. They have stingers. Stingers have poison.

Meerkats can eat scorpions without harm. They have **immunity**. They're not affected by scorpion poison.

Meerkats look for scorpions. They move quickly. They grab the scorpions. They bite off their stingers. They brush off the body in the sand. They remove most of the poison. Then they eat!

Meerkats eat other animals. They eat lizards, snakes, spiders, eggs, small mammals, centipedes, small birds, plants, and fungi.

Adults teach babies. First, they give them dead scorpions. Second, they give them weak scorpions. Third, they give them live scorpions.

Chapter ten

VULTURES

Vultures are scavengers. They eat dead animals. They eat **carrion**. That's the rotting flesh of animals. They rarely attack healthy animals. But they do attack sick animals. They attack injured animals. They're not picky eaters. They'll eat cooked, raw, or rotting meat.

They have amazing eyesight. Some have amazing noses. They smell death a mile away. They fly. They look for dead animals. They eat quickly.

Dead things can have dangerous germs. Dead things are deadly.

Vultures don't carry food to their babies. They throw up the food into the babies' mouths.

A little bit of the germs can kill humans. A little bit can kill other animals. Vultures have strong stomach juices. These juices kill harmful germs.

A group of vultures eating is called a wake.

Vultures have weak legs. Their claws are not sharp. But they have powerful beaks. They use their beaks to rip dead animals. They help each other rip the bodies. They often eat in groups.

They eat a lot. Then they have to sit for a while. They get sleepy. They have to digest their food. Many eat too much. They need to become lighter. Some vultures throw up. This is so they can fly.

They dig their heads into dead animals. They have bare heads. They have bare necks.

They walk on dead animals. Some vultures pee on their legs and feet. This kills germs.

WHEN ANIMALS ATTACK!

Wolves are known as man-eaters. Many stories feature the big, bad wolf. Three types attack humans. First are wolves that have never seen humans. Second are wolves that have gotten too used to humans. Third are wolves that have rabies. Rabies is a sickness. But most wolves don't attack humans. Wolves eat what they can to survive. Their perfect meal is large deer, moose, or elk. They kill as a pack. They gang up on their prey. They rip away legs. They rip at the guts. They wait for prey to fall down. Then they eat right away. They eat prey while they're still alive. They even eat dogs. They're related to dogs. But it doesn't matter. Wolves have bigger teeth. They have bigger bites.

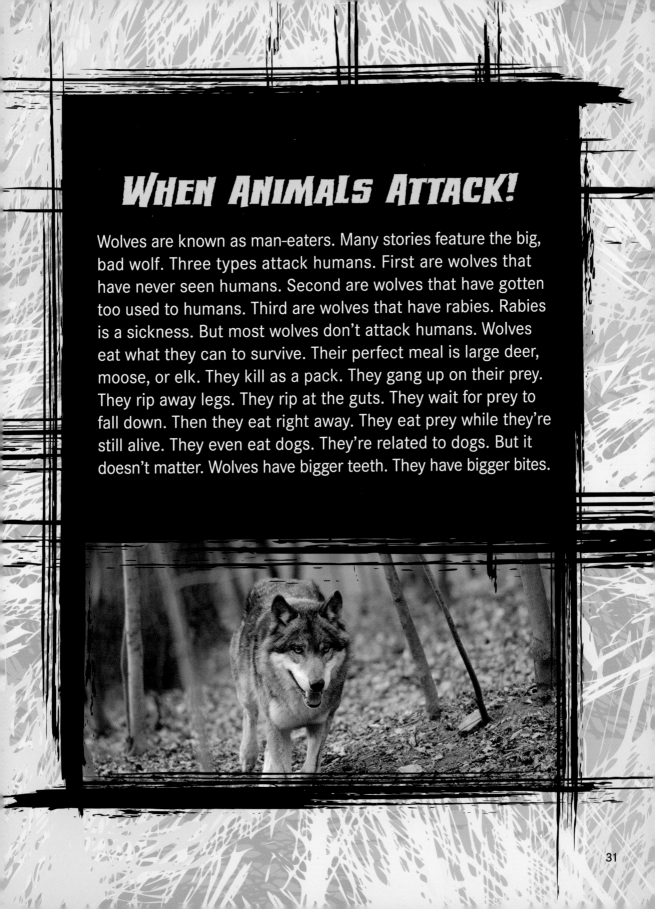

CONSIDER THIS!

TAKE A POSITION! Some humans use cleaner fish for their skin conditions. Do you think humans should use animals for their own purposes? Argue your point with reasons and evidence.

SAY WHAT? Animals' bodies are built for how they eat. Explain at least one way in which an animal's body helps it eat.

THINK ABOUT IT! Animals eat to survive. All animals are part of a food chain. Create a food chain with animals from this book.

LEARN MORE!

- Jenkins, Steve, and Robin Page. *Time to Eat*. Boston: Houghton Mifflin Books for Young Readers, 2011.
- Swanson, Diane, and Terry Smith (illustrator). *Animals Eat the Weirdest Things*. New York: Holt, 1998.

GLOSSARY

carrion (KAIR-ee-uhn) rotting flesh of animals

coral (KOR-uhl) rock-hard sea animals that stay in the same place

diet (DYE-it) what animals eat

digest (dye-JEST) to break down food and absorb it into the body

dung (DUNG) poop

groom (GROOM) clean

immunity (ih-MYOON-ih-tee) not being affected by something

microscope (mye-KRUH-skope) tool with a lens that makes small things look bigger

minerals (MIN-ur-uhlz) crystal substances

parasites (PAR-uh-sites) tiny living things that live on or in animals and feed off them

pincers (PIN-surz) claws

predators (PRED-uh-turz) hunters

prey (PRAY) animals that are hunted for food

reef (REEF) ridge of coral rocks

scavengers (SKAV-uhnj-urz) animals that feed on dead animals or plants

survive (sur-VIVE) to live, to stay alive

INDEX